Shapes

This book belongs to

_____

FS109009 Shapes

Name_____

Square

Color.

Trace.

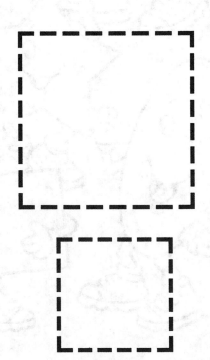

FS109009 Shapes

Name _____

Stacking Squares

Trace. Color.

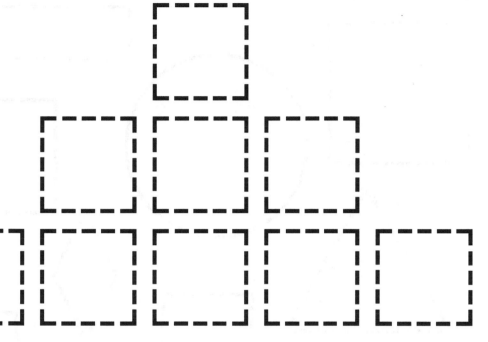

There are _____ squares.

Draw 4 squares.

Name _____

Searching for Squares

Color the squares.

4
reproducible

FS109009 Shapes

Name _____

Square Hunt

Color the squares.

5
reproducible

FS109009 Shapes

Name _____

Square Presents

Draw a line from each present to a square that matches in size. Color.

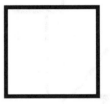

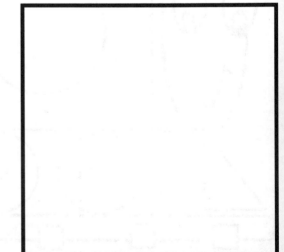

FS109009 Shapes

Name _____

Circle

Color.

Trace.

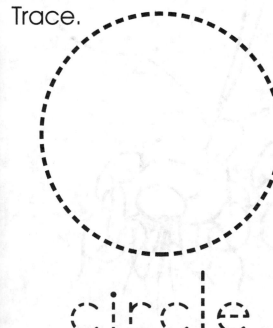

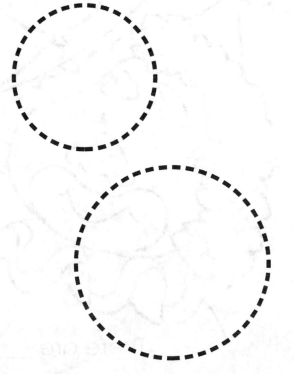

FS109009 Shapes

Name _____

Circle Fun

Trace. Color.

There are _____ circles.

FS109009 Shapes

Name _____

Making Circles

Trace. Color the grapes purple.

Draw 3 more grapes.

FS109009 Shapes

Name _____

Circle Search

Color the circles.

10
reproducible

FS109009 Shapes

Name _____

Round and Round

Color the circles.

FS109009 Shapes

Name _____

Triangle

Color.

Trace.

triangle

Name _____

Terrific Triangles

Trace. Color.

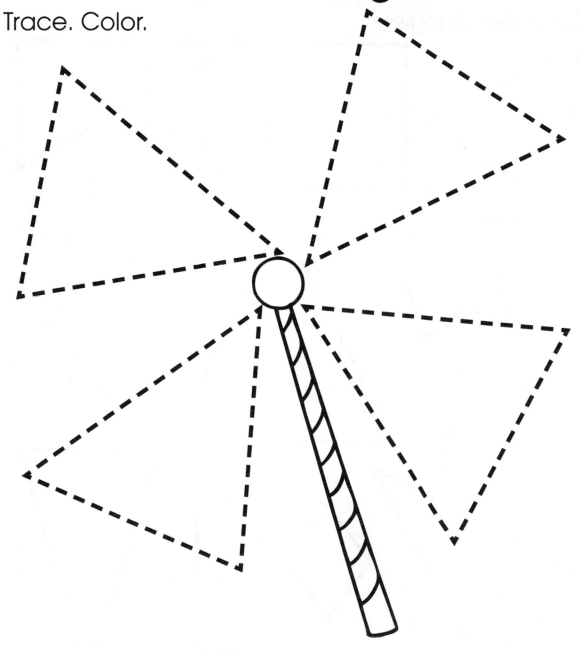

There are _____ triangles.

FS109009 Shapes

Name _____

Find the Triangles

Color the triangles.

FS109009 Shapes

Triangle Time

Color the triangles.

Draw 2 more triangles on the boat.

Big and Little Triangles

Draw a line from each face to a triangle that matches in size. Color.

Name_____

Rows of Super Shapes

Finish the pattern in each row.

Name _____

Rectangle

Color.

Trace.

rectangle

FS109009 Shapes

Name _____

Royal Rectangles

Trace. Color.

There are _____ rectangles.

19
reproducible

FS109009 Shapes

Name_____

A Rectangle Hunt

Color the rectangles.

20
reproducible

FS109009 Shapes

Name _____

Rectangle Fun

Trace. Draw 2 more rectangles on the ball.
Color the picture.

21
reproducible

FS109009 Shapes

Fantastic Flag

Use the code to color.

= red   = blue   ☆ = yellow

FS109009 Shapes

Name _____

Diamond

Color.

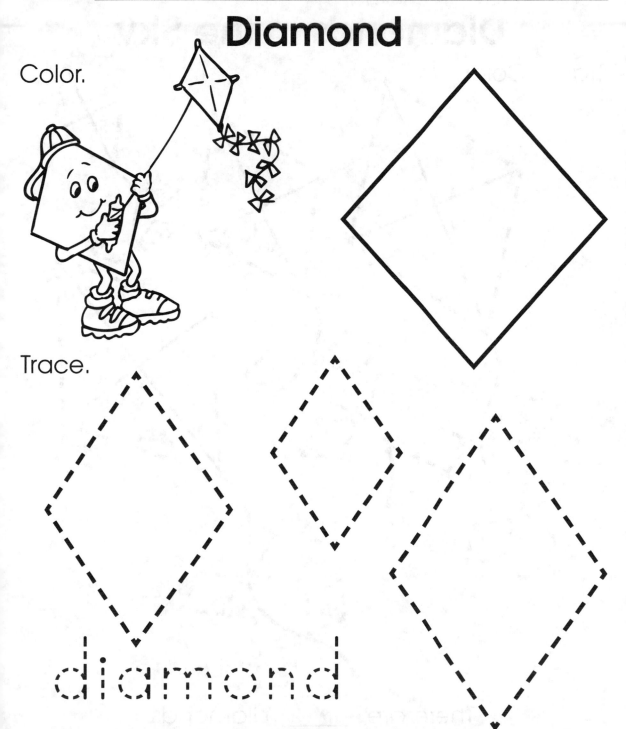

Trace.

diamond

FS109009 Shapes

Name _____

Diamonds in the Sky

Trace. Color.

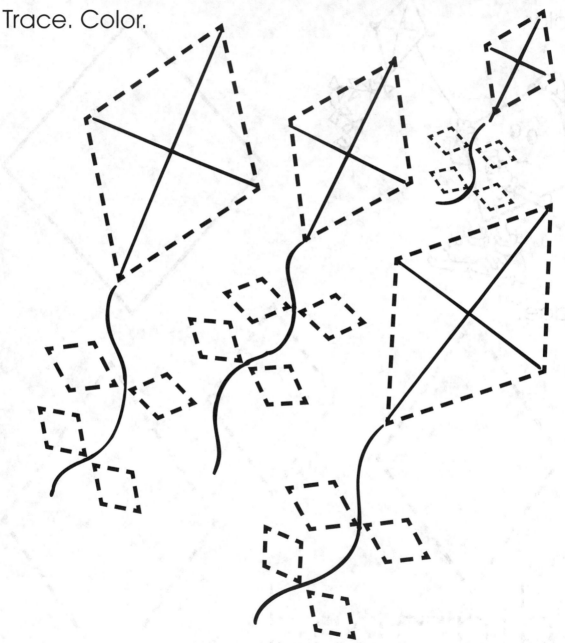

There are _____ diamonds.

FS109009 Shapes

Name _____

Dandy Diamonds

Color the diamonds.

25
reproducible

FS109009 Shapes

Drawing Diamonds

Color the small diamonds yellow.
Color the big diamonds green.

Draw 3 more diamonds in the picture.

FS109009 Shapes

Diamonds in Hiding

Find and circle 6 hidden diamonds.
Color the picture.

FS109009 Shapes

Name _____

Heart

Color.

Trace.

FS109009 Shapes

Directions:

1. Have your child cut out the shapes on page C. (Point out the octagon, as it may be new to your child.)
2. Have your child cut out the game board on page B.
3. Help your child match the cutout shapes to the shapes and names on the game board. (Shapes and words are color-coded.)
4. Encourage your child to look at each shape and say it for you.

For more fun, let your child cut out the shapes, tie a piece of string to each one, and tie them to a hanger to create a mobile. Your child could also add pictures of other objects of the same shapes to the mobile.

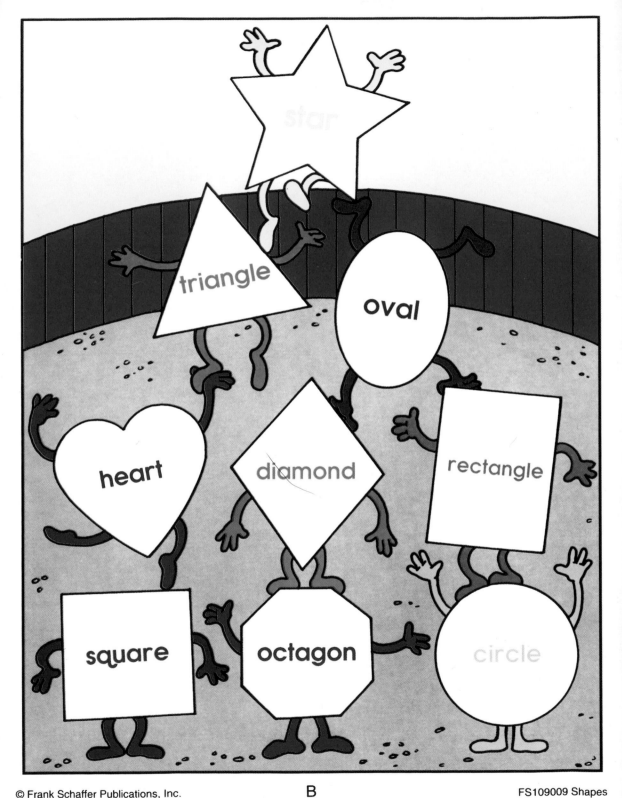

B

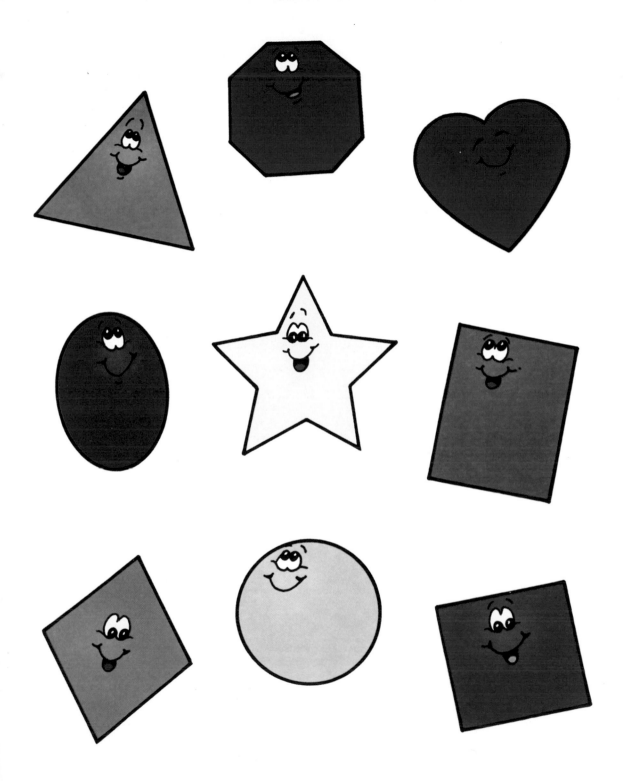

C

D

Name _____

Happy Hearts

Trace. Color.

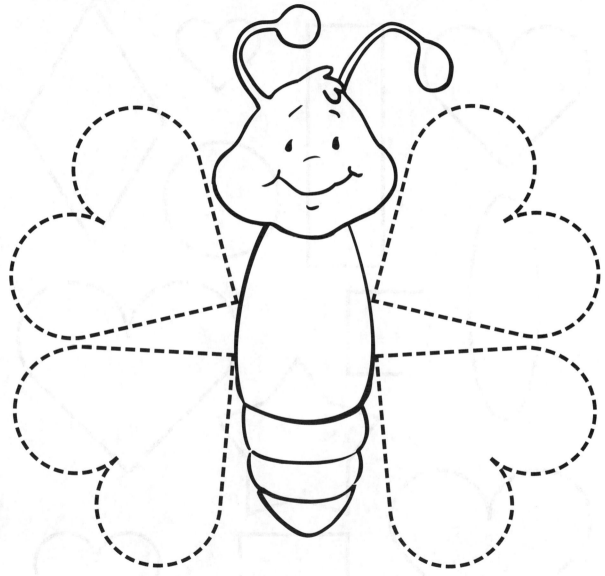

There are _____ hearts.

FS109009 Shapes

Name _____

A Heart Hunt

Color the hearts.

30
reproducible

FS109009 Shapes

Handy Hearts

Color the hearts.

Draw 1 heart in each hand.

Name _____

Heart Matchup

Draw lines between hearts that match in size.

FS109009 Shapes

Name _____

Perfect Patterns

Finish the pattern in each row.

33
reproducible FS109009 Shapes

Name _____

Star

Color.

Trace.

star

FS109009 Shapes

Name _____

Super Stars

Trace. Color.

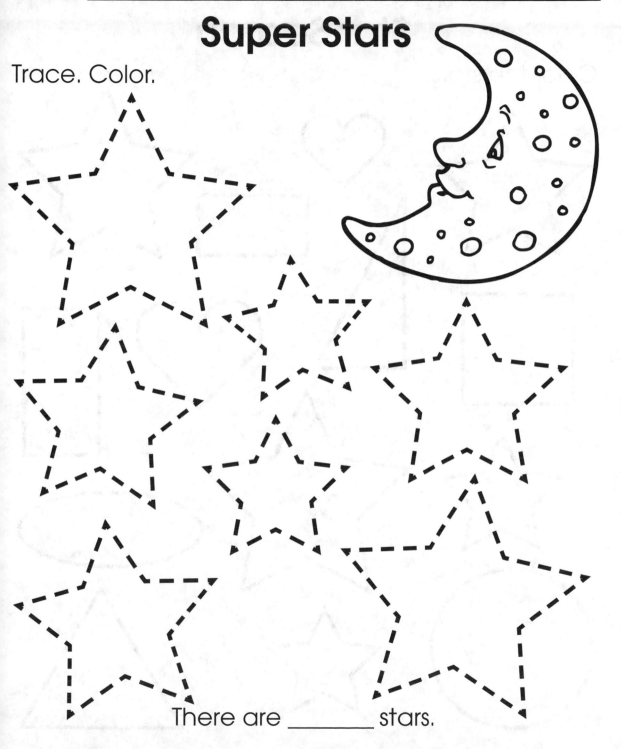

There are _____ stars.

FS109009 Shapes

Name _____

Star Search

Color the stars.

FS109009 Shapes

Floating Stars

Color the stars.

Draw 2 more stars on the balloon.

A Soccer Star

Find and circle 5 hidden stars.
Color the picture.

FS109009 Shapes

Oval

Color.

Trace.

oval

39
reproducible

Name _____

Oval Eggs

Trace. Color.

There are _____ ovals.

FS109009 Shapes

Awesome Ovals

Color the ovals.

41
reproducible

FS109009 Shapes

Name _____

Only Ovals

Color the ovals.

Draw 2 more ovals in the picture.

FS109009 Shapes

Name

Sizing Up Ovals

Draw lines between ovals that match in size.

FS109009 Shapes

Name _____

Finishing Up

Finish the pattern in each row.

FS109009 Shapes

Name _____

Park Play

Color. △ blue ◇ red ⬭ green
○ yellow

FS109009 Shapes

Name _____

Shapes All around Us

Draw lines between matching shapes. Color.

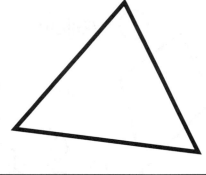

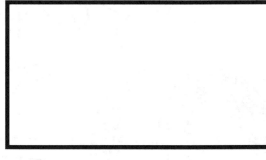

FS109009 Shapes

Super Shapes

Draw lines between matching shapes. Color.

Name _____

Super Skater

Color. ☆ blue ♡ red ☐ yellow

☐ orange

48
reproducible

Name _____

A Shapely Beach

Find and color the shapes.

☆ purple   ○ yellow   ◇ blue   ▭ red

49
reproducible

FS109009 Shapes

Name_____

Word and Shape Matchup

Draw a line from each word to its shape.

circle

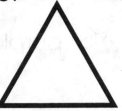

square

triangle

rectangle

FS109009 Shapes

Name _____

Word and Shape Matchup

Draw a line from each word to its shape.

diamond

heart

star

oval

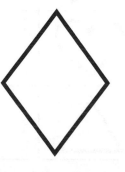

FS109009 Shapes

Shape Graph

Look at page 53. Color one box in each row for each shape you see.

◯					
▢					
⬭					
▯					
◇					
☆					
♡					
△					

53
reproducible

FS109009 Shapes

School Is Fun

Find and color the shapes.

☐ red   △ blue   ♡ green

◯ yellow   ◇ purple

FS109009 Shapes

Name _____

Shaping Up

Draw a picture. Include as many shapes as you
can in it. Outline each shape in blue.

FS109009 Shapes

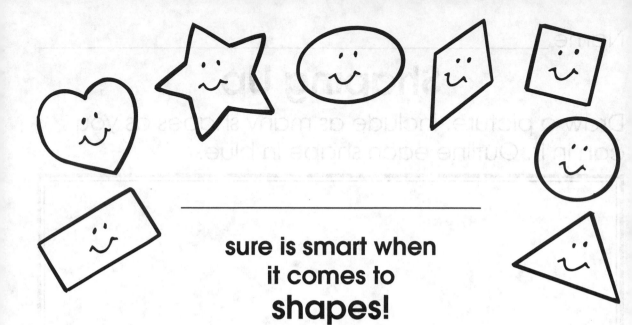

_____

sure is smart when it comes to
shapes!

Great job!

_____
signature

_____
date

56
reproducible